Someone You Love H

A Child's Guide to Understanding

By Robin Martin Duttmann

Illustrations by Kalpart

Strategic Book Publishing and Rights Co.

Strategic Book Publishing and Rights Co., LLC
USA | Singapore
www.sbpra.com

For information about special discounts for bulk purchases, please contact Strategic Book Publishing and Rights Co., LLC. Special Sales, at bookorder@sbpra.net.

ISBN: 978-1-68181-949-5

This book is dedicated to the many nurses and volunteers at The Windsor

Regional Cancer Center. You are true inspirations.

Also for Dr. Hamm, Dr. Heartwell, and Dr. Hermiz with sincere thanks.

With love for my greatest support my Mum, and for Ken

– I love you now and always.

Useful Websites:

Myevent.com – Will assist with creating social media events for fundraising

Kemoshark.com – A kid friendly zone with games and information presented in a downloadable comic book form

Cancer.org – An adult website with current information

Kidshealth.org – Serving both parents educators and children

Someone you love has cancer
And that's a frightening thing
It can make your heart hurt
With the uncertainty it brings

It might be Mom or Grandma
Your grandpa or your dad
A brother or a sister
And it's bound to make you sad

The more you know what to expect
The less you might be scared
So here's a little book for you
To help you get prepared

5

Just know that though it's difficult
There really is a plan
A team of doctors and nurses
Will lead with gentle hands

It may have started with a lump
In Mom or Grandma's breast
She may have had a mammogram
Which is just a little test

As men and women get older
They have a colonoscopy
Again it's just a little test
To make sure they're cancer free

Now if it comes back negative
They say, "You're good to go
We'll see you in a year or two"
And they will send you home

But should it come back positive
More tests will come their way
They might need extra hugs from you
To get them through their day

Cancer is not contagious
You cannot catch it too
It is not passed on like a cold
With germs from them to you

It is cells within the body
That are not working right
The good cells and the bad cells
Start to have a big, fat fight

Cancer cells are cells that grow
At a really fast pace
They can cause a tumor
That invades a healthy space

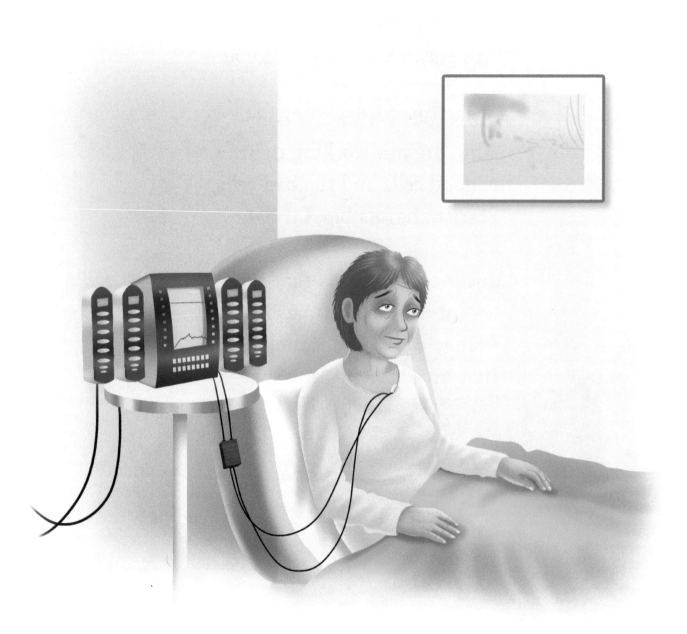

If malignant, there are choices
You will come to see
Of surgery, radiation
Or chemotherapy

Surgery is when doctors
Make a big decision
To take out a tumor
With a little incision

Radiation is a laser
Like in a video game
It's aimed at the tumor
So it'll never be the same

It will shrink the tumor
Hopefully until it's gone
If so then your loved one
Will be able to move on

If the tumor is shrinking
But does not go away
Chances are your loved one
Will need chemotherapy

Chemotherapy is a big word
For a type of medicine
It comes in different forms
Like pills or injection

Chemo has some side effects
That may give you a scare
Some people lose their fingernails
Their eyebrows or their hair

In time their hair will grow back
But sometimes until then
Some people chose to wear a wig
Until they are on the mend

Cancer can make them grouchy
And make them feel very weak
It can make them sleepy
And not want to eat

It may make them gain weight
It may make them lose
But one thing it won't do
Is change how they feel about you

It might make you feel scared
Worried or alone
Talk about your feelings
With whoever is home

Chances are that they
Feel the same way too
Comfort one another
Love will see you through

It may take a long time
For the cancer to be gone
But once it is it's likely
You'll sing a happy song

18

Sometimes things don't go right
Sometimes things go wrong
We'll wrap our arms around you
So you know where you belong

So be brave my friend
We know that you are
We are thinking of you
We hold you in our hearts

The Memory Box

Purpose:

Your Memory Box is a place to put your valuables for the purpose of remembering life events or memories you treasure.

What might go in Your Memory Box? Anything small that will fit in the box that has special meaning to you

Examples: photographs, letters or poetry, postcards or brochures, shells or special stones, a bottle of sand- collected from the beach, movie stubs or tickets from special outings like a play or concert, a coin or token from a subway, souvenirs from places you've visited, newspaper clippings, pressed flowers, a small bottle of perfume, recipes, a bible verse or prayer, a song, a small stuffed animal or toy, a hand print, a clipping of hair, a lost tooth, a disk of you singing, a video, a music CD

Materials

1.   Basic Materials: wooden box or shoe box with a lid, tissue paper, a variety of ribbons

2.   Tools and Accessories: hot glue gun and sticks, Modge Podge

Glue, paint brushes, scissors, containers to hold the Modge Podge, a drop cloth or old tablecloth

3.   Extras: glitter, speciality paper, stencils, stickers

Step 1. Cover your wood box in a layer of Modge Podge to help give it a smoother surface to work with. Wait 15-20 minutes for it to dry.

Step 2. Lay the dry box out on the patterned paper, pretty side down. Using a pencil, lightly trace the outline of the box onto the paper.

Step 3. Once completed, try wrapping the paper around the box to see where the excess paper needs to be cut. Your best bet will be to cut the corners at 90 degree angles, making sort of a cross or "plus sign" (+) design. Once you're happy with the layout, trim the excess paper.

Step 4. Start spreading a medium layer of Modge Podge all over the box and sticking the paper to the box. Wait 15-20 minutes for this to dry once completed. After it has dried, check to see if there are any spots where the paper is lifting and add more Modge Podge there.

*Another choice you have is to use tissue paper or magazine clippings cut into square Modge Podges and put onto your box

Glossary of Terms

Abnormal – Not normal, worrying

Benign – Not harmful

Cancer – A disease caused by abnormal cells in a part of the body

Chemotherapy – Medicine usually injected into a port or intravenous picc line, but can come in pill form as well

Colonoscopy – A test that helps Doctors to look inside the intestines for tumors

Hospice – A home providing care for the sick, especially the terminally ill

Injection – A shot, needle

Malignant – Life threatening

Picc Line – Is a hollow tube that a doctor or nurse puts into a vein. It is used to give chemotherapy and other medicines.

Port – A disc made of plastic or metal that sits just under the skin. Medicines are given through a needle that fits right into the port.

Radiation – The treatment of disease, especially cancer, usually using X-rays

Remission- A decrease in or disappearance of signs and symptoms of cancer

Surgery – The treatment of injuries by incision (cutting). Surgery for cancer usually means cutting out the bad, or cancerous cells or tumors

Transfusion – Using donated blood, typically to boost low blood counts

Tumor – A swelling of a part of the body, a lump caused by an abnormal growth of tissue, it may be benign or malignant

Fundraising

Fundraising gives children a sense of control. They are actively doing something to make someone's day brighter, or to better the situation. Involve them in the process as much as possible. The success of an event is usually determined by two things: organization and awareness

Organization: Every ship needs a Captain, let it be you.

Have a meeting, ask for volunteers, and assign jobs according to each one's strengths. Write down who is doing what and offer guidance along the way, being careful to allow them as much control as possible. Remember the acronym K.I.S.S. – Keep it simple silly. Check back often to be sure that if the event is larger, things are in order.

Awareness: Let the "cause" remain first and foremost.

Create empathy by making others aware of the situation for which you are holding the event. If it's a student in your class, say so. If it's for an ill parent or sibling of a child in your neighbourhood say that. Personalize it so that others may relate, and will contribute knowing they've done something to help you, by helping the "cause."

Make signs and posters and create social media events where applicable. Call local media: radio, television and newspapers. Contact local businesses and ask them to help by providing things such as a venue, water and small snacks, such as granola bars, in exchange for their name being listed as a sponsor.

Give the Children as much ownership of these events as possible. Remember it's about giving them some sense of control in an otherwise chaotic time.

Finally: When all is said and done remember to thank everyone involved from the sponsors to the children and volunteers, as well as to the media. Use this time to educate by telling a little about the specific types of cancer your loved one has been stricken with and reminding people of signs and symptoms related to this disease. Inform them where the donated money will go and how much was raised. If a website was created for future fundraising, give them that information, as well. If there is a Facebook page or newsletter to update on someone's progress, share it.

Fundraising Ideas: Old Fashioned Lemonade Stand: Remember it's not about the *what*, but about the *cause*. Anyone will pay a dollar for a small glass of lemonade as long as it's for a worthy cause.

Bake Sale: Send out a letter one week before the event requesting donations and volunteers. Send out reminders the day before.

Spring Bulbs: Sell bulbs or daffodils – most nurseries will give a reduced price for inventory if going to a good cause.

Used Book Sale: Petition neighbours, family and friends to donate their used books and organize a used book sale.

Art Sale: Give each child a canvas and paint and allow them to create a painting. Hold a silent auction on meet the teacher night. The paintings, of course, go to the highest bidder.

Hold a "Loonie for Licence" Day – This is a day where each child will pay a set amount on a scheduled day to either receive privileges, like chewing gum, or to be allowed to skip out on certain things, such as homework for the day. Most kids will pay a dollar to bring their favorite stuffed animal or wear pyjamas all day too.

Walk-a-thon or Read-a-thon: This is where people give donations in exchange for a promise that each student will walk a certain number of steps, or read for a certain amount of time. (See below for Donation Letter.)

Pasta dinner: This is a much larger event that will obviously require more time, preparation, and adult volunteers. The steps remain the same however. Hold a meeting, get volunteers, get sponsors, advertise, host, and then thank. Involve the children by allowing them to do what they can by creating advertising and making lists. Pasta dinners on their own typically do not raise much money, but if you sought silent auction items from local businesses, trades, and artists, your donations will increase significantly. (See below Silent Auction Form and Request of Donations letter.)

Create a Go-Fund-Me Account. With the evolution of Social Media, people are fundraising in new ways, where funds are generated solely by creating and acquiring donations online with social media awareness being the foundation of success.

Donation Letter

Dear_____

I'm writing on behalf of _____
_____. As you may have heard we are holding a fundraiser on
_____, for _____.

I am seeking donations in the form of _____
_____.

A team of volunteers could pick these items up by_____
_____. In exchange your name would appear on advertising
as a sponsor for this event.

I can be contacted at_____ if you have any
further questions. Thank you in advance for supporting this worth-
while cause.

Sincerely,

Silent Auction

Item: _____   Value: _____

$ Increments: Item Increases by $_____ Increments

Name _____

Address _____

Phone Number _____ Email _____ Bid $_____

_____

_____

_____

_____

_____

_____

_____

_____

_____

Highest Bid: Total $ Amount Due: _____